D0604092

T 155018

J   cl
746.46
STA
Stalcup, Ann
American quilt-making:
stories in cloth.

DESERT FOOTHILLS LIBRARY
P.O. BOX 407
CAVE CREEK, AZ 85327
488-2286

DEC 0 6 1999

American Quilt Making: Stories in Cloth

Ann Stalcup

The Rosen Publishing Group's
PowerKids Press™
New York

DESERT FOOTHILLS LIBRARY
P.O. BOX 4070
CAVE CREEK, AZ 85327
488-22__

To my husband, Ed, who shares my love of folk art and travel

Published in 1999 by The Rosen Publishing Group, Inc.
29 East 21st Street, New York, NY 10010

Copyright © 1999 by The Rosen Publishing Group, Inc.

All rights reserved. No part of this book may be reproduced in any form without permission in writing from the publisher, except by a reviewer.

First Edition

Book Design: Resa Listort

Photo Credits: pp. 4, 8, 9, 11, 17, 18, courtesy of Vickie Paullus at Mountain Mist; p. 6 by Resa Listort; pp. 7, 13, 16 © UPI/Corbis-Bettmann; p. 12 © Joe Viesti/Viesti Associates, Inc.; p. 19 © Martha Cooper/Viesti Associates; pp. 20, 21 by Christine Innamorato.

Stalcup, Ann, 1935-
    American quilt-making: stories in cloth / Ann Stalcup.
        p.   cm. — (Crafts of the world)
    Includes index.
    Summary: Traces the history of quilting and describes the various kinds of quilts made in the United States. Includes a suggestion for a quilt-making project.
    ISBN 0-8239-5334-3
    1. Quilting—United States—History—Juvenile literature. 2. Quilts—United States—History—Juvenile literature. [1. Quilting. 2. Quilts. 3. Handicraft.]
I. Title. II. Series: Crafts of the world (New York, N.Y.)
TT835.S685 1998
746.46'0973—dc21
                          98-6464
                          CIP
                          AC

Manufactured in the United States of America

Contents

Quilts Through the Centuries

People all around the world have been quilting for thousands of years. A quilt is two pieces of cloth sewn together with padding, called batting, in between. The batting is held in place by small, neat stitches that often make a design.

Egyptians wore quilted clothes 5,000 years ago. Around 1200 AD Dutch and English ladies discovered the warmth of quilted clothing, and they made blankets the same way.

Patchwork quilts were made from squares or rectangles cut from fabric scraps or old clothing. **Immigrants** (IH-muh-grints) brought quilts from Europe to the New World. Women who quilted in the United States began to create new designs. Quilts have become one of America's **contributions** (kon-trih-BYOO-shunz) to the world of folk art.

◀ Quilts have been around for hundreds of years. Over those years, new designs, patterns, and colors have been developed.

Desert Foothills Library

Quilting Bees

For more than 300 years, American women who quilted kept baskets of fabric scraps by the fireplace. Every night a woman would sew a few pieces of scraps together. Eventually she would have pieced together the top of a quilt. Once the top was completed, it was time for a quilting bee.

A quilting bee was like a quilting party. As many as ten women would gather around a large quilting frame. They would hand-stitch the top of the quilt to the back with small,

neat, stitches. In between the top and the back was the layer of batting. Because these quilts were made from scraps that were pieced together, they were called **piecework** (PEES-werk) quilts.

Quilting bees were a time for women to get together and talk about family and friends. ▶

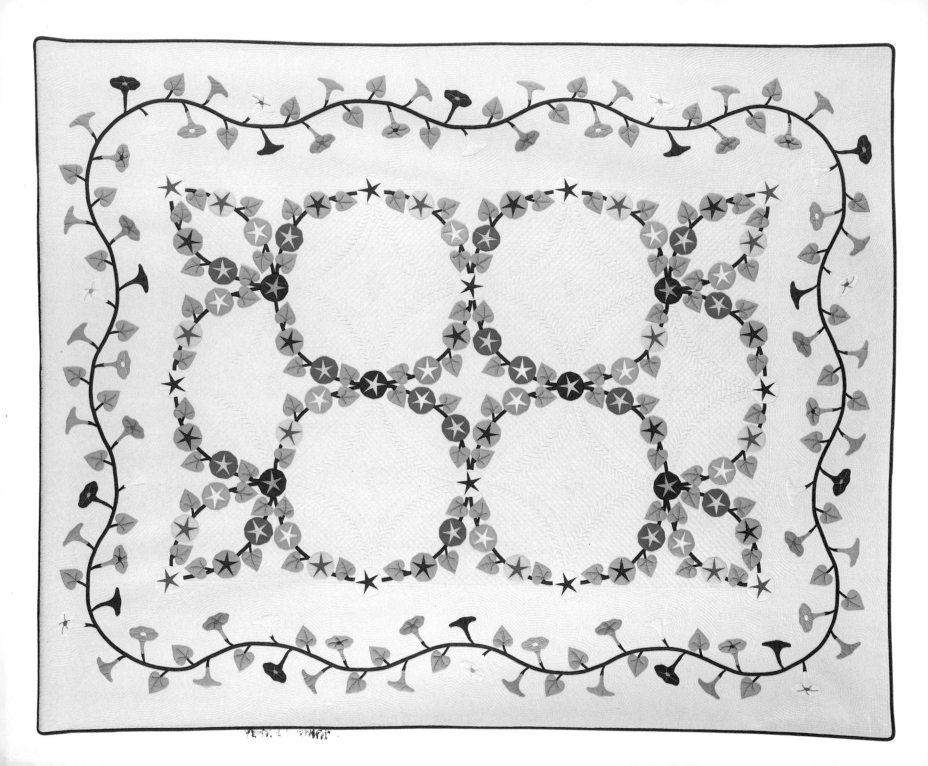

The Move West

In the early 1800s American families began to move to the western **frontier** (frun-TEER). Their quilts showed the new places they saw and people they met. Every quilting pattern had a name. Some new designs had names such as wagon wheel, log cabin, cactus flower, pine tree, flying geese, country roads, and north star. Sometimes the same **geometric** (jee-oh-MEH-trik) design had two names, depending on who made it and where she lived.

New quilts called picture quilts were also made during this time. Picture quilts have designs that look like pictures, such as flowers or animals. These designs were **appliquéd** (a-plih-KAYD), or stitched, onto the top of the quilt instead of being pieced into the quilt.

◀ This picture quilt has a design called morning glory. The flowers on the quilt look like the real flowers called morning glories.

Desert Foothills Library

Album Quilts

Another kind of quilt is called an album quilt. Each square of an album quilt shows an event in a family's life. Squares may show a baby's birth, a new house, or a move to a new place. Years ago album quilts were a lot like today's photo albums. For example, a mother might make one for her daughter as she grows up.

Other album quilts were made by friends for a family that was moving. Each square was different and might show the quilter's home, family, or farm. Designs were appliquéd onto the quilt. The quilt was proudly hung on the wall of the family's new home. The quilt would remind the family of their friends.

This album quilt shows the history of the thirteen ▶ colonies that became the United States.

I only regret that I have but one life to lose for my country

Nathan Hale - Huntington L.I. N.Y. - 1776

LIBERTY

N J

3

PROSPERITY

FREEDOM OF

RELIGION

RHODE ISLAND

LIBERTY BELL BEING CARTED TO ALLENTOWN SEPT. 18, 1777 PA.

PAUL REVERE'S RIDE

MASS.

New Hampshire Live Free or Die

1776

1776   1976

PENNSYLVANIA

Canada

New York State

Lake Ontario

Marriage of the Waters
1825
ERIE CANAL

Susan, S. Caldwell
Charlestown,
Mass

Friendship Quilts

Friendship quilts, or **autograph** (AW-toh-graf) quilts, are made for special events, such as weddings. Friends and family members each decorate a square. They may **embroider** (em-BROY-der) the bride's name, the date of the wedding, and sometimes a message. Today people often use special fabric pens to sign their square. Some autograph quilts have a large panel in the middle for the date of the wedding and the names of the bride and groom.

Friendship quilts are made for other events too, such as the birth of a baby. These quilts often become family **heirlooms** (AYR-loomz). They are special to a family and are passed down from parent to child.

◄ An autograph quilt allows a person to include her name on the quilt she is creating for someone she loves.

AIDS Memorial Quilt

A special friendship quilt was started in 1987. Each panel of this quilt is made to remember someone who died from AIDS. This quilt was created to make people more aware of this terrible disease. Anyone who has lost someone to AIDS can make a panel. If a person would like to make a panel but can't sew, a quilting bee is organized to help that person. Each decorated panel includes the name of the person with AIDS and the date he or she died.

The AIDS quilt is still growing. More than 43,000 3' x 6' panels and fabric walkways cover an area as big as 25 football fields! The quilt is so big that it can no longer be opened in one place anymore. It has to be split up.

It can be hard to visit the AIDS quilt. Some people feel sad when they see how many people have suffered and died from this disease. ▶

Amish Quilts

In 1683 many Amish people left Europe and settled in Indiana, Ohio, and Pennsylvania. They lived in simple homes with little furniture. They farmed with basic tools, and used horses and buggies instead of cars. The Amish still live this way today.

The people who lived near the Amish taught them how to quilt. The Amish are known for their tiny stitches and **intricate** (IN-trih-kit) designs. The designs they create are usually geometric. The colors that the Amish use make their quilts **unique** (yoo-NEEK). Purple and black are used much more than the **calicos** (KA-lih-kohz) used by many quilt makers.

Amish family members from age 4 to 80 work on each quilt. Quilt making is a family project.

These Amish women are creating a quilt with a design called the "wedding band."

Hawaiian and Hmong Quilts

In 1820 Christian **missionaries** (MIH-shuh-nayr-eez) traveled from the United States to the Hawaiian Islands. The missionaries' wives taught Hawaiian women to make quilts. But Hawaiian ladies had no baskets of fabric scraps. Using bright new fabrics, the Hawaiians appliquéd one bright color onto another. They created large designs that were one-of-a-kind. Designs often looked like island plants and fruits such as the hibiscus, pineapple, and breadfruit.

The Hmong are a people from Asia. Hmong **refugees** (ref-yoo-JEEZ) tell their family histories on quilts. The quilts show peaceful farms and dangerous journeys. They show boat, train, and plane trips to the United States. Many Hmong quilts have bright colors, such as blue, purple, red, and black.

Hawaiian quilts (above left) are known for their flower designs. Hmong and other Asian quilts (right) are known for their bright colors. ▶

Cut-out Quilt:

You will need:

glue
ruler
scissors
construction paper
    in lots of colors

1. Cut the construction paper into squares about 5 inches by 5 inches, and triangles about 5 inches by 5 inches by 6 ½ inches.

2. Arrange the squares and triangles on a piece of 8 inches by 8 inches construction paper. Mix up colors and shapes to make a bright and interesting pattern.

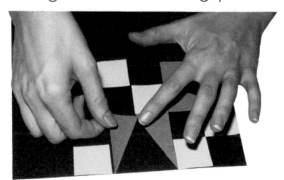

3. Glue the squares and triangles to the construction paper.

African American Quilts

African American women have been quilting for hundreds of years. Many began quilting as slaves. Using their masters' old clothes, slaves would make quilts that told the history of their families. These quilts were passed down through families.

Quilting is still a large part of African American **culture** (KUL-cher). Many African Americans believe that quilts made by their mothers, grandmothers, and aunts have special powers. It's believed that the **spirit** (SPIR-it) of the quilt maker stays in the quilt forever. That spirit watches over whoever uses the quilt to stay warm.

Quilts are not always handmade anymore. But those that are have become a form of art. They are very special to the families that own them. Quilts are even hung in museums. They are an American living history.

Glossary

appliqué (a-plih-KAY) One material attached or stitched on top of another.

autograph (AW-toh-graf) A person's signature.

calico (KA-lih-koh) Cotton fabric with small, flowered designs.

contribution (kon-trih-BYOO-shun) Something that is given.

culture (KUL-cher) The beliefs, customs, art, and religion of a group of people.

embroider (em-BROY-der) To stitch designs into cloth for decoration.

frontier (frun-TEER) The last edge of settled country, where the wilderness begins.

geometric (jee-oh-MEH-trik) Having to do with lines, triangles, and circles.

heirloom (AYR-loom) A valuable and interesting object handed down through a family.

immigrant (IH-muh-grint) A person who moves to a new country from another country.

intricate (IN-trih-kit) Complicated.

missionary (MIH-shuh-nayr-ee) A person sent by his or her church to teach other people his or her religion.

piecework (PEES-werk) Sewing together leftover pieces of cloth into a design.

refugee (ref-yoo-JEE) A person who leaves his or her own country to find safety.

spirit (SPIR-it) A person's soul.

unique (yoo-NEEK) One-of-a-kind.

Desert Foothills Library

Index